A glance back at
Newnham-
on-Severn

The earliest known photograph of Newnham High Street, with horses, carts and farm implements in the road. Note the lime trees in the centre; such a feature of the town, they were planted circa 1862, mainly at the instigation of M.F. Carter, which dates this picture to about 1870. The view of the Lower George Inn is not yet obscured by the clock tower.

by
Humphrey Phelps

**Black Dwarf
Publications**

Acknowledgements

I am greatly indebted to a trio of Newnham ladies, namely Barbara Allsopp, Nita Gould and Anne Lloyd, for their invaluable assistance. Thanks for providing photographs go to Barbara Allsopp, Trevor Askew, Clifford Clark, the Dean Heritage Centre, Nita Gould, Caroline Phelps, the late Alec Pope, Helen Watts and Neil Parkhouse. The rest are from the author's own collection.

THE NEWNHAM DAFFODILS 512

Postcards featuring the brief annual display of the Newnham daffodils were very popular and this example, with the street bathed in sunshine, dates from the late 1940s. They were planted during the 1930s, mainly at the instigation of Dr. H.J. Selby who became Newnham's physician in 1928.

> **This book is dedicated to the memory of Jimmie Prosser**

'Newnham is by far the prettiest and most pleasurable town on the banks of the Lower Severn.
It perches itself on a cliff overlooking a fine stretch of sand.'
R.W. Beckingsale. *Companion into Gloucestershire.* 1939

Black Dwarf Publications
is an imprint of **Black Dwarf Lightmoor**
Unit 144B, Lydney Trading Estate, Harbour Road, Lydney, Gloucestershire GL15 4EJ
To view all our titles and to place orders log on to: www.lightmoor.co.uk
Series Editor: Neil Parkhouse. Tel: 01594 844789 or email neil@lightmoor.co.uk

Printed by The Alden Group, Oxford

~ A short history of Newnham-on-Severn ~

Newnham was one of the five ancient Boroughs of Gloucestershire and the only one west of Severn. In the Middle Ages, it was conveniently situated for hunting in the Forest of Dean and thus much visited by kings – William II, Henry I, Henry II, Edward II and Edward III all came to Newnham. Both Henry I and Henry II signed charters here. Henry II (who maintained an anchorage here for a while) signed a Charter in 1158, which was witnessed, among others, by Thomas the Chancellor – Thomas Becket, who had become Chancellor four years earlier. Becket was then at the zenith of his pomp and glory. In 1171, Henry II met Strongbow (Earl of Pembroke) at Newnham before they proceeded to Milford Haven and thence to Ireland with a large army. The Sword of State, the second largest in England, is reputed (but doubtfully) to have been given to Newnham by King John.

By the 13th century, Newnham was a borough town with the right to return a Member of Parliament. This distinction was a rather dubious one as far as local people were concerned, however, as they had to pay for the privilege. Accordingly, they petitioned to be relieved of this financial burden and Newnham's parliamentary representation was discontinued.

During the Civil War, Sir John Winter of Lydney, who was a staunch Royalist, kept a garrison at the Church and at '*the fort adjoining*'. The day after the affray at Westbury, Colonel Massey marched to Newnham to deal with Winter's men and gained possession of the town without any opposition. Then one of Winter's men, '*one Tipper, a most virulent papist*', fired a barrel of gunpowder in the church and severely singed a great number but killed none. Enraged, Massie's men set upon Winter's men, killing twenty and taking about one hundred prisoner. Mabel K. Woods, in her *Newnham-on-Severn* (1912) wrote '*We have in Newnham an old tradition that in pursuit of the Royalists some of Massie's men fell into the river while fighting; and being unable to swim in their heavy armour, were drowned, but not before they had cursed the town of Newnham and prayed that its women should not live. And for many years after, every man in the town was, sooner or later, a widower.*'

'*The fort adjoining*' may have been the Newnham castle or merely the defences thrown up by the Royalists. The castle itself could not have been a very substantial one but the *Victoria County History* (Vol. X) states, '*There is no good reason for doubting that the three-sided earthwork with ramparts and a ditch on the high ground at the south end of the town was, as it appears to be, a Norman castle rather than part of the defence thrown up in 1643.*' It was certainly an ideal site for a castle. There was a great and mysterious fire around 1300 and the town was subject to raids by the Welsh and by Foresters. During the 14th century, a band of armed men bearing lighted lanterns and torches set fire to the rectory.

Undoubtedly, Newnham was settled because of the comparative ease of crossing the river at this

Part of an old print, showing the Bear Inn, centre, at the bottom of Passage Lane; it was also called Passage House. By the mid 18th century the borough and manor courts of Newnham were held at the Bear, in 1831 the Commissioners of Woods held sittings there and by 1856 petty sessions also. When it was for sale in 1837, together with the ferry and fishery it was also the Posting House. '*I entered the Bear Inn at Newnham, with a good appetite and found a round of beef just taken from the pot, which I strove to devour, and likewise a gooseberry pie.*' (Hon. John Byng [Later Lord Torrington] Diary June 1781.)

point and its importance and prosperity in former days was due to the river. A ferry was recorded in 1238 and, a little upstream by Hawkins Pill, the river could be forded. There was, said Samuel Rudder in 1779, *'a very safe passage or ferry over the river for horses and carriages, and ford passable at low water.'* Thomas Rudge in 1803 wrote, *'From this town is one of the passages over the river, which is perfectly safe, and may be made in almost every state of the tide for men, horses and carriages. Near to this place a rock rises so near to the surface at low water, that horses and carriages are conducted across with great safety, by a guide, without a boat. But to those who are unacquainted with the line of the ridge, the attempt is attended with extreme danger, as the rock does not gradually shelve off, but precipitates suddenly to a great depth on either side.'*

As a port, Newnham's main trade was timber, bark and hides to Bristol, and, during the 16th and 17th centuries, with goods to Ireland, chiefly glass and cider – the cider made in quantity in the district had a renowned reputation. By then the Crown had appointed Newnham one of the creeks of the port of Gloucester. There was also a considerable trade in shipping timber from the Forest of Dean at this period. In the mid 18th century, Robert Pyrke built a new quay, with cranes and warehouses. Goods from Birmingham were carried down by river and transshipped to larger vessels for consignment to London. Coal from the Forest of Dean was brought to the quay by horse and shipped from Newnham. So was bark for Ireland and Rudder wrote *'Newnham bids fair to be a flourishing little town.'* Other cargoes carried by the two-masted, square-rigged Newnham brigs included earthenware, cast iron and ironmongery arriving from the Midlands, with verdigris and vitriol being exported from the town's chemical works.

Ships were being built at Newnham in the 18th century. A brig of 180 tons, the largest built so far up the river, was launched in 1764; fourteen years later, a Newnham ship of 600 tons was launched. Ship building continued until the beginning of the 19th century, at which time Newnham's port gradually lost trade to Gatcombe and to Bullo. A tramroad to the latter opened in 1809, tunnelling under Haie Hill, so coal from the Forest went straight to the harbour and quays constructed between 1808 and 1818. The fate of Newnham's port was finally sealed when the Sharpness to Gloucester ship canal opened in 1827.

There was a market in the 12th century and customs on cloth were collected in the town during the 14th century. There was a market-house by the early 17th century, where market tolls were collected. In 1771, the lord of the manor was ordered by the court leet to remove the remains of the market-house and the pound. A new pound was built in 1839, on its present site and one of the few still in existence in the district. It was used to pen straying animals until 1928. The town is recorded in 1220, 1584 and again in 1603 as having a prison. A market was held every Friday from the 16th century but by 1740 the corn market was in abeyance for some time, due to the bad condition of the roads, and within two or three decades the weekly market had declined. Two fairs were held each year, on St Barnabas Day (11 June) and St Luke's Day (18 October). In the early 1800s, the fairs were mainly for horses and cattle but by 1912 they had also become pleasure fairs. During the period of the First World War, the sale of livestock ended, although the pleasure fairs continued until 1928.

In 1310, the church stood perilously close to the river which was undermining it. Eventually it had to be taken down and a new church was built. The living was a perpetual curacy. During the 16th century, the churchwardens had presented that their curate was an unlawful gamer and failed in his duties, whilst the one who followed him was excommunicated for failing to pay a subsidy. His successor was a former monk from Flaxley Abbey, whilst later, in the early 19th century, a curate who became very popular was found not to be in holy orders and to have defrauded some local inhabitants of money, so was imprisoned for forgery.

It was alleged that opposition to the religious revival – which meant Nonconformity –

Mrs Grice of Haie Lodge, who was aged 70 in 1958, recalled the story behind this scene as told by her grandmother. '*Certain people of consequence in Newnham were rather elated after a wedding and removed the seats from the Green which were carved in the shape of 'queer beasts'. They carried them away and threw them into the river. Another version says they burnt them. When the removal was notified to the local authorities a reward of £5 for information was offered, the resolution being solemnly voted by the persons responsible for the removal. The reward was never claimed.*' This sketch also shows the church in its pre-1875 restoration state.

Castle House (formerly Branksome) on the right was a Gloucestershire Banking Company branch as the sign indicates; it moved to different premises in the 1840s, so this illustration is prior to that date. Later, the house became the home and offices of M.F. Carter, Solicitor.

in and around the Forest reached its height in Newnham. John Horlick, a leading member of the Independents (and incidentally, of the Horlick family of Ruardean who later invented the beverage known as Horlicks) stated: '*About 1797 a Mr Collins, a clergyman of the establishment, attempted to preach an evening lecture in a dwelling house, but the service had not proceeded far before the windows were all broke, the people dispersed and the family obliged to leave the town.*' More damage was alleged. Later, the Independents' pulpit was thrown into the Severn and a house registered in 1838 for Wesleyan preaching was wrecked.

An Independent Chapel was built in 1826. The Independents later became Congregationals and a new Congregational Chapel was opened in 1864. The Good Templars had a hall in what is now known as Station Street in 1877, which later became a church hall and then a Masonic hall. In 1839, the Church of England had a school in the High Street – the inscription, now faded, can still be seen on the lintel. The Independents had a school by the chapel. A new National School was built in Church Road in 1867; two years later it had an attendance of over one hundred pupils, with another twenty attending evening school.

When Newnham was a borough, it was governed by a mayor and burgesses, although later it was said the mayor and aldermen had no authority over the town. The court leet was held in October generally at the Bear but sometimes at the Upper George (sometimes the Ship). From 1894, the town was governed by the Newnham Urban District Council, which had twelve members until 1935, when it became part of Gloucester Rural District Council – when Newnham had two councillors to represent the parish.

The banking industry had quite an effect on Newnham's later history and on the town's façade. There was a Savings Bank by 1830 and, a few years later, the Gloucestershire Banking Company opened a branch at Castle House (formerly Branksome). In the early 1840s, the bank moved to premises in the High Street (Bank House). S. W. Woods became manager in 1870, with Stephen Haddingham, his nephew, as assistant. In the mid 1880s, Woods and Haddingham left to join the Bristol & West of England Bank, which opened a Newnham branch at the Beeches. The Gloucestershire Banking Company was then taken over by the Capitol & Counties Bank and new premises were built (its sign over the doorway still exists) next to the Bank House. The Bristol & West of England also built new premises, adjoining the Beeches, before Woods retired in 1888, to be succeeded by Haddingham. Lloyds Bank took over the Bristol & West of England's Newnham branch and moved further up the High Street. Lloyds also took over the Capitol & Counties Bank and so for a while Newnham had two Lloyds branches. When Haddingham retired, the two were merged. Haddingham died in 1951 aged 97.

Newnham does not look its age – F.W. Baty in his *Forest of Dean* (1952) called Newnham the '*Lady-Who-Never-Grows Old*', because many of the old houses were re-built or re-fronted during the 18th century. From the Whetstone Brook at the north end of the town to the church at the south end the road rises seventy-five feet. It has also been claimed that a row or even two rows of houses stood on the wide bank between the two roads in High Street. This is mere fancy, there is no foundation for this claim but nevertheless it has crept into some publications.

Another mistaken claim relates to the black bricks or blocks which can be seen in several buildings and walls in Newnham. They are found in many buildings near the Severn (Frampton has some good examples) and right up beyond Gloucester. Local legend will have it that they are made of glass slag from the Newnham glass works, an error repeated in some local history books. In fact the blocks are of copper slag and probably came up the river as ballast from the copper works at Swansea. Although there was a copper works at Redbrook, it is unlikely that it was a source of blocks all along the Severn environs. William Marshall stated in 1780: '*Below Gloucester the roads are made with slag copper dross.*'

On the Whetstone Brook there were two watermills. The upper corn mill was near Culver House, the lower one, called Butchers Mill, was near where the railway station was built. Tanning was carried on in and around Newnham for several centuries – bark came from the Forest of Dean and the last tannery, at Underhill, continued until the 1920s; its buildings survived until the late 20th century. Spinning, weaving and tanning were done at the parish workhouse during the early 19th century. In 1835, Newnham and several more parishes became part of the Westbury Union workhouse, administered by a Board of Guardians.

High Street and the Severn from the air around 1930.

The Nailyard, off Station Street, was out of use by 1879. The Chemical Works or verdigris factory, sited up the lane by Unlawater House, was the cause of a riot in 1774 when local people thought it was consuming locally grown food. This was a few years before the Bread Riots, in which the town was not involved directly. In 1831, '*Capitalists, bankers, professional and other educated men*' constituted over ten per cent of the total number of the adult male population in the town. There were ten farmers in the parish, then twelve by 1856 and fourteen in 1927 – all of them employing labour.

Like many small, largely self reliant communities of the 19th and early 20th centuries, the people of Newnham were quite capable of looking after themselves in more ways than one. When Dr. H.J. Selby first came to the town, he lived in lodgings and looking through the window he saw a crowd of people marching by. Intrigued, he joined them and came to a house on fire. To his amazement, people were carrying away chairs and other household items. Wondering what sort of place he had come to, he learned the next day that the fire was in the house of a certain tradesman and was told, '*He robbed people over the years and now they're getting their own back on him!*'

Newnham has quite a penchant for name changing. Passage Lane became Severn Street, Back Street became Church Road, Hill House became Unlawater House, the Ship Inn became the Upper George and the Rose Inn became the Ship Inn. Station Road (formerly Curriers Lane) was home to the Masonic Hall, which was originally a Church of England Hall opened in 1879 and a Temperance Hall. It became

	1608	1902	1931	1939
Auctioneers		1		
Bakers/Confectioners		2	2	1
Banks		1	1	1
Bark Merchants	1			
Beer Retailers		2	2	
Bootmakers/Repairers	5	3	1	1
Butchers	1	2	2	2
Chemists		1	1	1
Clockmakers/Repairers		2	3	2
Coopers	2			
Drapers		3	2	1
Feltmakers	1			
Fishmongers		1	1	1
Grocers		3	3	4
Glovers	1			
Inns	2	6	6	6
Ironmongers		1		
Millwrights	1			
Newsagents		1	2	2
Printers		1	1	1
Pinners	1			
Post Office		1	1	1
Ropemakers		1	1	
Saddlers/Harnessmakers		1	1	
Various Other Shops		6	5	7
Tanners	1			
Tailors	3	2	1	1
Weavers	2			

a Masonic Hall around 1925 and was enlarged. In the 1940s there was also a plastics factory in Station Road but a fire put an end to that enterprise.

The table, above, gives a breakdown of the commercial enterprise of Newnham over the centuries. Of all the trades and shops in this table, only the chemist, the printer, Baileys Stores, the Post Office, and the Victoria, Ship and Railway Inns have survived until 2003. Apart from this, the High Street looks very much the same as it did sixty or seventy years ago. Only the constant stream of heavy traffic mars the perennial charm of Newnham, which is still by far the prettiest and most pleasurable town on the banks of the Lower Severn. Finally, it should in fairness be mentioned that, according to various Gazetteers and also the Ordnance Survey, the town's name is officially Newnham; however, the author and most locals much prefer Newnham-on-Severn, a most apt and descriptive title which distinguishes it from all the other Newnhams around the country.

A group of Good Templars under the verandah by the Victoria Hotel around 1910. The Forest of Dean proved to be fertile ground for the Temperance Movement and by 1857 there was a strong Temperance group based in Newnham. Meetings were held in premises in Severn Terrace, now converted into cottages. Later, they were held in a new building in Station Road.

We begin our tour proper of Newnham at the river with this view of Newnham Pill, the mouth of the Whetstone Brook, circa 1900. There was a small quay here until the Pill was culverted in 1850. One of Newnham's glass works stood near here and so did the Anchor Inn, which together with some ancient houses were demolished by Mr Wilde, a solicitor in the town who lived at Hill House (later Unlawater). This photograph, which was taken by J. Philpotts, the local chemist, shows great activity at the Pill.

Newnham's port trade began in the 16th century at least but it grew as quite an important transshipment port from the 18th century, where upriver cargoes were transferred into smaller vessels and vice versa. Looking north, this view shows one of the warehouses at the former quay; the buildings survive today converted into a dwelling. They were partly built with black slag blocks. This was also the site of the shipyard.

A dramatic view of the river at Newnham in February 1917. It is recorded that the river was thick with ice like this for the first two weeks of the month and several postcards were issued showing the phenomenon. The Severn and many other English rivers were frozen for the first time since 1895. The warehouse, top left, places the exact location as Newnham Sands, a shallow part of the river which would thus have frozen over more easily. Compare this with the top view on page 40.

The river has for centuries been fished, mainly for salmon and elvers, providing a meagre living for some and a supplementary income for others. This scene, showing long netters at work, dates from circa 1930.

Salmon Fishing

A view of Undercliff and the church from across the river. Tom Phillips lived in the second cottage on the left. Mr and Mrs Phillips had fifteen children and eventually the family occupied both cottages. However, they fell into disrepair in later years and were demolished around 1970. Over the centuries, the river has eroded the cliffs at this point, taking away a pathway running round the cliff and up to the church; the path used to more or less follow the line of the rock strata visible here.

Looking up the Severn towards Broadoak, in the distance, from the riverbank just below the cottages, with various small craft belonging to Tom Phillips (and possibly others) pulled clear of the water. The nearer rowing boat, which looks freshly painted, may have been a spare ferryboat, whilst the others were used mostly for fishing. These craft would all have been locally built. This postcard, by Bailey Bros. of Cheltenham, dates from circa 1910.

~ 9 ~

Above: A rather splendid photograph showing Tom Phillips (standing) about to leave with a boat load of passengers in about 1910. The dress indicates a party out for a Bank Holiday river trip on, perhaps, rather than a simple crossing. Phillips retired as ferryman in 1927 aged 70 years and died in 1939. He lived across the river at Arlingham before moving to Newnham. In 1889, two of his young sons were drowned while paddling in the river. They were out of their depth before anyone could save them.

Centre: A busy view of the ferry and the Nab circa 1908. The large vessel was for carts and animals. '*Dr Brown reports that in Gloucestershire this month the Ferryman at Arlingham Ferry recalled having seen in his youth as many as four hundred head of Welsh cattle waiting on the Welsh side of the ferry to be carried over this side.*' (George Sturt Journals, Sept. 1908)

Bottom: With cart, horse and several passengers already on board, the large ferryboat is seen here nearly ready to leave Arlingham in about 1902. The ferryman is carrying Mrs Runicles to the boat in the usual manner. The photograph was taken by her husband, the Runicles family being on a day out from their home in Cinderford.

The newly discovered photographs on this page, taken around 1890, provide a graphic illustration of the ferry at work. Even the menfolk using it had to be carried across the mud, top left. Top right, we see a cart being manoeuvered down the slipway. The next picture shows it being carefully rolled onto the large ferryboat *Albert Edward*, with the horse already onboard keeping a watchful eye on the proceedings and the ladies in their Victorian dress also looking on rather anxiously. Phillips knew what he was about, however, and in the bottom picture the craft is seen out in the river with the cart balanced across amidships – a typical arrangement on ferries such as this all round the country. All this, of course, was worth the effort to cut out the 20 mile round trip via Gloucester. The ferry could be very busy on occasions; a local newspaper said that one Whit Monday 1,000 people used it. Phillips's stepson William Hayward became ferryman on his retirement. Hayward had a small shed by the ferry where he repaired boots and shoes. He died in 1948 aged 65 years.

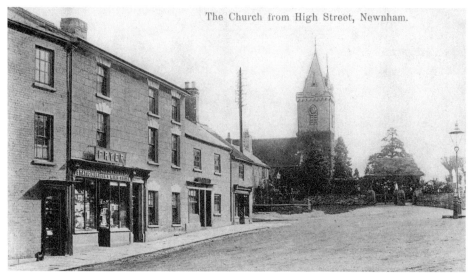

The Church from High Street, Newnham.

Newnham has been unfortunate with its churches. An earlier one was undermined by the Severn and had to be dismantled and another was subsequently built, on the present site, in 1380, on land given by Humphry de Bohun. That church was completely restored and enlarged in 1875 at a cost of £4,600 but in February 1881 it was destroyed by fire. The fire was discovered at 5 a.m. by Charles Beard on his way to work. Within an hour the Newnham Fire Brigade had arrived. There was some difficulty in obtaining water but about 100 men and women formed a chain and passed buckets of water from adjacent wells. Brigades of the Liverpool & London, Globe and the Norwich Union came from Gloucester but the fire had got a great hold and soon the roof fell in. The church was

rebuilt at a cost of £4,430. On the left is William Sidney Fryer, bookseller, printer, stationer and stamp distributor. Fryers were here from 1841 until 1912. The view below, one of Tilley's of Ledbury's coloured postcards and dating from circa 1908, shows the ivy-covered house on the left which was demolished in 1910-1. The present churchyard wall was built in 1914.

Above: The charming lych gate to St. Peter's church happily still survives today. This view, looking through the gate to the Upper High Street and dating from about 1905 was published by Albert Blanton.

28/6/27

Newnham from Church Tower

These two general views of the top end of Newnham were taken from the elevated vantage point of the church tower by Cinderford photographer R.G. Gibbs. The sender of the card above thoughtfully penned a date on it, giving us a reasonably accurate indication of when the picture was taken. This is quite early for Gibbs – most of his postcards seem to date from the 1930s. Note the range of vehicles on view, including what looks to be a home made pick-up truck on a Ford chassis – the handiwork of Watts of Lydney perhaps? For the second picture, Gibbs has turned the camera ninety degrees. Church Road runs in front of the houses in the foreground and past the National Schools. Brightlands School is just behind. There looks to be a bit of a mist coming in off the river too.

Newnham from Church Tower.

The Victoria Hotel dates from the early 18th century. When the hotel was for sale in 1840, there were daily London/South Wales coaches stopping and the sale advertisement said the hotel was in full business, had accommodation and that '*the salubrious air of Newnham*' was the best in the kingdom. It also went on to mention that, in all probability, a bridge across the river would be erected opposite the hotel. In 1877 plans were revealed for a bridge from Newnham to Arlingham at a cost of £25,000 but they came to nothing and the only attempt to bridge the river here was the unsuccessful floating bridge of the late 1940s. On the first landing of the Victoria's fine staircase there was, until quite recently, a small glass panel set in the window depicting the fable of the Grasshopper and the Ant: '*The Grasshopper came unto the aunts [sic] and demanded part of the come whereupon they did aske what he had done in the sommer and he said he had sang, and they did saide, 'If you song in the sommer then daunce in the winter'*. Talbot's dray is making a delivery to the hotel in this circa 1900 view and behind it is the saddler's shop (later A.L. Sheen, baker). Note the fine gas lamp and post, a feature in many of these photographs. The advertising card for the Victoria Hotel, below, dates from the 1930s.

ESTABLISHED ABOUT 1620.

This old-fashioned First-class Residential Hotel offers superior accommodation to Tourists, also Motorists, who are visiting the Forest of Dean and district, and Wye Valley.

Luncheons Daily.
Table d'Hote on Sundays 1 to 2-30.
Separate Tables.
Good Plain English Cooking.
Afternoon Teas.

· TERMS :

2 GUINEAS TO 3 GUINEAS PER WEEK.
SPECIAL WEEK-END.
18/6 EACH PERSON.

Excellent Garage and Pit.
Week-end Tickets, Friday and Saturday.
Illustrated Booklet Free.

Manageress :
Miss GREENSMITH.

Beautiful views of the River Severn.

VICTORIA HOTEL,
NEWNHAM-ON-SEVERN, GLOS.

Two views of the High Street from near the Dean Road junction, looking south, above, around 1911 and north, below, about 10 years later. The two gentlemen in the top picture are standing on the stone setts marking the start of Severn Street. First on the left, below, is the butcher's shop which was formerly the Red Lion. Dr. Selby had it converted into a dwelling house on his retirement. Next is the shoe shop, then the Ship Inn and, a little further on, the grocer's shop which was once kept by the Playsteads. The Market House probably stood on the bank by the old Lamb & Flag, and stalls may have been placed on the bank on fair and market days. The lime trees have matured well in the 60 years since their planting.

High Street, Newnham, Glos.

This postcard looking view down the High Street was published around 1912. Note how quiet the road was in those days. In his memoirs, Jimmie Prosser (1895-1974) wrote of '*the wide, tree lined, empty and absolutely silent village street.*' The children could play with their hoops in the road without fear – wooden ones for girls, iron hoops for boys. On the right can be seen Burnett's confectioners and next door the Britannia Inn. Behind the first tree on the left was James and Mary Playstead's grocery shop; they were also drapers, and wine and spirit merchants. William Charles Hadley had the business in the 1920s and Thomas George Allen in the 1930s. The tall building behind the drinking fountain is the Manor House.

The Britannia Inn, midway down the High Street, is not listed in the 1902 edition of *Kelly's Directory*, although elsewhere there is reference to it as being tied to Wintle's Brewery at Mitcheldean in 1903. Albert Barnes, hairdresser, further down, is in the 1902 *Kelly's* and was still at the premises in 1931.

Both of these views date from a similar time, around 1905. Carefield's Temperance Hotel, Refreshment & Dining Rooms, the building in the centre with the white frontage, later became a Ministry of Labour Employment Exchange and then a Butcher's shop. Next door, the Police Station opened in 1873 and beyond that, Blanton's Plumbers & Decorators which had begun at another site in Newnham in 1839. At its centenary, Fred Blanton was the proprietor. He was also a photographer (his photography room was at the rear of this shop) and a well-known figure in the district, wearing a trilby hat at a jaunty angle, bow tie, mauve silk shirts, plus fours and brightly polished shoes of the best quality.

The premises of J.A.A.W. Fox, watchmaker, jeweller and grocer, at Dean Corner feature prominently on this card which Fox published himself. He was a German Jew and, because of his accent, was nicknamed 'Vatchy Fox'. A familiar chant of Newnham children many years ago was '*If you vant to buy a vatch, buy a vatch, if you don't vant to buy a vatch, take your face away from my vindow.*' The shop later became a fish shop and then a newsagents and in recent years it has housed an insurance brokers.

Lower High Street around 1910 with Lloyds Bank on the right. This had originally been opened by the Bristol & West of England Bank, a company subsequently taken over by Lloyds. The premises ceased to be used as a bank in the 1920s, when Newnham's two Lloyds branches were merged. At one time in the 1930s the premises were occupied by a Mr Williams, a greengrocer, who during the summer took deck chairs on a handcart for hire at the Cliff. William Shortman's ironmongery shop was next to the bank and Samuel Shortman, clockmaker, once occupied the adjoining premises.

Mrs Sarah Blanton's shop sold hardware, china, toys and all manner of things. She was mother to Reginald Blanton who owned the garage just up the street; he and Fred were half-brothers. Next door is Bank House, built for the Capitol & Counties Bank and which later became one of the Lloyds branches. At the far end of the street stands the house known as the Beeches. Once a private residence, the lower part to the left was added by the Bristol & West of England Bank in the latter half of the 19th century. In the 1930s the Beeches was in use as an orphanage but it is now demolished.

A fine view of Lower High Street around 1912, with a motor parked near the bottom of the street and the addition to the Beeches house to accommodate the bank on the right. Unlawater House features in the background. The demolition of the Beeches and widening of the road at this point has significantly altered this aspect today, although the houses on the left still remain.

The staff of the Post Office, posed in front of the building for a group photograph in the early 1920s. Those men who served in the First World War have chosen to wear their medals so it must be some sort of special occasion. Second from left is William Carefield and the postman on his left is Harold Stevens. This property is now occupied by the Public Library, whilst the Post Office is on the other side of the High Street.

Henry J. Burnett,

Baker, Cook,

Confectioner & Caterer.

Home - Made Veal and Ham and Pork Pies, Ices, Jellies, &c.

Game Pies, Hams, Tongues, Boar's Heads, Boned Turkey, Galantines, &c. to order.

RICH WEDDING CAKES.   Hovis & Turog Bread.

Luncheons and Teas Catered for.

HIGH STREET, NEWNHAM-ON-SEVERN.

Above: Philpotts the chemists. James Richard Philpotts was at this shop in 1906, probably around the time this view was taken. He was also a professional photographer, one of three in Newnham, which is why it was well recorded pictorially. Another photograph of Mr Philpotts shows him with a number of pigeons on the pavement, so presumably he was also a pigeon fancier. There was a Philpotts, chemist in Newnham in 1815. In 1853, Joseph Philpotts was recorded as a chemist, druggist, grocer and tea dealer, and purveyor of horse and cattle medicines in the town. By 1914, Bower & Sons were the chemists in Newnham and Percy Waterhouse had the chemist's shop in 1939.

Right: This photograph of Henry J. Burnett's bakers and confectioners shop in the High Street was taken in about 1914. The property itself is called Kingston House.

Above: 'Price late Morse' butchers in about 1905. Morse in fact had been the previous butcher here and obviously a good one with a name worth perpetuating. In the doorway stands the butcher, Albert Price. His father Edwin Price had also been a butcher in Newnham. The boy is Albert's son but the figure on the right is unknown. Albert used to buy fat lambs at Arlingham and bring them back on the ferry. Albert Price & Son retired from the shop in the early 1940s. This property was formerly the Lamb & Flag Inn and the Chepstow coach started from here. Then, in 1864, Henry Bailey, blacksmith at the old Lamb & Flag, let out the front shop and buildings for a slaughter house, to Henry Stinson the butcher.

Right: The shop of T. French, Boot and Shoe Maker, High Street around 1912. Mr French is remembered as having also travelled round the district selling shoes in the 1930s.

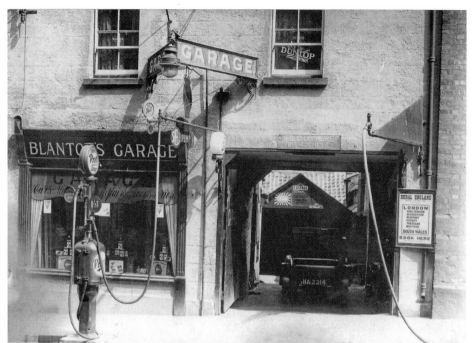

Blanton's Garage in the 1930s. The notice above the doorway reads 'Fill up here with Shell', although the only pump on view dispenses Pratts petrol at $1/5^1/_2$d a gallon – about 8 pence! However, the hose on the right connects to another pump out of picture. The board indicates that Proprietor Reginald Blanton (Fred Blanton's brother) also acted as agent for Rural England Motor Coaches Ltd.

William Stafford took over this business at the top of the High Street from William Fryer in 1912, which is when this picture was taken. By 1922 William Wheeler owned it. Today the shop and printworks are still in the hands of the Wheeler family and the shop front is virtually unchanged from this view.

After the First World War, the Town Hall became the Comrades Hall, with a wartime Field Gun outside. By 1939 it had become the home of the Newnham Club and during the 1940s films were shown here. In the late 40s, a troupe of travelling actors came for a week or so, putting on a different play each night and up to 1950 the Forest of Dean Divisional General Election count was held here.

An early photograph of the Lower George, Commercial Hotel & Posting House when still in its prime, probably dating from the late 1890s. The view also illustrates a couple of different modes of horse-drawn transportation – the vehicle on the left is a gig, the one on the right a brougham.

The True Heart Inn, seen here in 1899, is now Sparkfield House. James Page, the innkeeper, was coachman to Sir Charles Dilke MP. He was also the grandfather of Jimmie Prosser who was born at the True Heart. 'Mr Jimmie' as he was always called, was a much-loved and flamboyant Newnham character. In the 1914-18 war he served in the Gloucestershire Regiment as a private. Severely injured on the battlefield at the Somme, he was paralysed for a long time but eventually recovered sufficiently to ride a bicycle and also find employment which took him away from Newnham.

Above: Soldiers' Club, First World War. They are posed outside Burnett's shop with their banner attached above. During the war there were refreshments and a good fire here for servicemen.

Right: Miss Annie Ball's shop in the High Street; she was still at the shop in 1939. It sold a great variety of goods as can be seen from the window, including the *Chronicle* and *Journal* newspapers. The shop closed many years ago but the frontage is virtually unaltered, as with many other of Newnham's ex-shops.

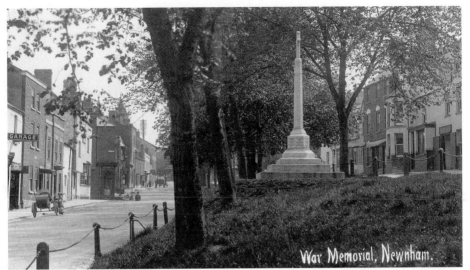

This view of the cross, erected to commemorate the men of Newnham who fell in the First World War, was taken by R.G. Gibbs around 1930. Note the motorcycle and sidecar combination parked on the left outside Reginald Blanton's garage.

On the immediate left in this 1940s view is Mansion House. Mr Clifford had a rope walk down to the river behind here. He brought the wrought iron porch and railings from Cheltenham in the early 19th century but the house is much earlier. In 1902, Anne Clifford was the ropemaker. The shop above once belonged to Roberts & Philpotts who, in 1851, advertised that they could supply ball gowns and gentleman's neckties for the annual Newnham Ball. Later, Henry Preece had the drapery business and the property. In 1871, he tried to sell this and other property but was still there two years later, opening a Cocoa Tavern next door which became the new meeting place for the Temperance Society. In 1902, Preece became part owner of the Ferry. In 1906, Frank Martin was proprietor of the Cocoa Tavern. At the time of this photograph there was a cafe here as well as a grocery shop. Just above is a barber's pole and above the barber's shop there was a gymnasium. Leslie Williams was the barber here and, to begin with, he used to cycle out from his home in Gloucester.

Looking down Upper High Street in the late 1940s, with John H. Jones & Co., grocers and drapers, and once also corn and flour merchants, on the left. During the 1930s, 40s and until their retirement in the 1950s, this business was run by the three Misses Jones. Miss Emmie Jones was a keen rose grower but so was a man on the other side of the street. Both carefully watched Peter the horse in Mr Hinds milk float because both had shovels at the ready to scoop up Peter's droppings for their roses. The shop was perfect, a delightful grocers of the sort that unfortunately no longer exists.

The Winter of 1947 hit the Forest hard, as with most of the rest of the country, and is still well recalled as a result. This photograph of snow piled up along the High Street illustrates how bad it was, with scenes such as this lasting for weeks on end. The Upper George Inn, on the right, is one of the oldest buildings in Newnham. Formerly called the Ship Inn, it was legally a detached part of the Hundred of St Briavels and outside the jurisdiction of the Newnham Justices. The Justices of St Briavels were unlikely to brave the miry roads to Newnham in search of miscreants, so it became a refuge for criminals and debtors, in what was called the Sanctuary Room. The bad state of the roads to Newnham was the main reason for the demise of the town's market. During the 1940s, the Upper George on Saturday nights was filled with local people and Land Girls from a hostel just outside the town. With the piano playing, laughter and singing, Saturday nights at the George were jolly nights. The inn closed around 1970 or soon afterwards.

Looking up the street from in front of the Lower George Inn, on the right, with the Congregational Chapel, built in 1864 of local stone in the Gothic style, in the centre. It had seating for 350 people and a 1 acre cemetery to the rear, added in 1884, which was administered by a Burial Board.

Lower High Street circa 1910. The house, first right, was once the Union Inn. Up the street, on the left, is Mornington Terrace, built by Tom Goold in the 1860s. He named it Claremont Terrace, having already built Claremont House just above, but it was later changed. Tom Goold and his brother Alfred owned the Soudley Iron Works and two mines which they sold for £20,000. Tom had a house in the High Street which he enlarged and, as he was Lord of the Manor, he named it Manor House. He died in 1879, aged 49 years. For 28 years he was also a solicitor in Newnham, in partnership with M.F. Carter. The wall, left, was demolished together with The Beeches around 1968.

Two views of the Town Clock and Lower High Street, both taken around 1912. The Clock Tower, 60 feet high, was erected in 1875 at a cost of £280. The money was obtained by public subscription, on the initiative of local banker S. W. Woods. His daughter, Mabel, wrote a history of Newnham. Bailey's Stores is second on the right in the top picture and Dr. H.J. Selby lived in the house with the bow windows when he was the town's physician. The picture above is the work of a firm called Young & Cooper, who hailed from Teddington, in Middlesex, as is the bottom view on the previous page. They did not venture into the Forest but published several cards of Newnham, Broadoak and Westbury. The view below is by Will Phillips of Gloucester, who did cover the Forest as well.

Looking up Severn Street (formerly Passage Lane) about 1920. On the left, the Bear Inn (at the bottom of the street) the garden of which ran right up to the rear of the High Street. The cottages on the left were built during the 1860s. The tall building, top right, is the Upper George Inn.

Looking down Severn Street leading to the ferry.

The Telephone Exchange at No. 5 Severn Street around 1910, with telephonist Miss Margaret Ferris standing in the doorway. Her mother was a midwife. The first telephone exchange in Newnham in 1899, referred to as the public call office, was situated in the house of Henry Hobbs, a veterinary surgeon, at No. 1 High Street. Including Hobbs, there were five subscribers. In 1906 the National Telephone Company Ltd took a twelve year lease on No. 5 Severn Street. By 1923, William Ferris is listed as a bootmaker in Severn Street, probably at these premises.

The field in the foreground of this circa 1906 view of Station Road belonged to Anselm Bailey's father. Sheep sales used to be held here, hence the pens. The sales were advertised to start at 12 noon, with the railway putting on suitable trains, the Up train arriving at Newnham Station at 11.55 a.m. and the Down train at 12 noon. Anselm Bailey and his wife kept Bailey's Stores on the corner of Station Road. He was the local carrier and coal merchant and, with his horse, was a familiar sight.

Station Road was formerly named Curriers Lane, because leather was dressed and coloured after tanning at works situated here. There were tanneries at Ruddle and by Hawkins Pill; the remains of the sheds at the former disappeared comparatively recently. Before it moved to Upper High Street, the Ministry of Labour Employment Exchange was along here. During the 1930s and 40s, the Railway Inn, down the other end, was run by a trio of Misses Jones, who were very strict over the language and behaviour of their customers. Note the gas lamp – the gas works were also in Station Road.

The main line of the South Wales Railway from Gloucester to Newport opened on 19 September 1851, although it was not until the following year that trains ran throughout, with the completion of the bridge over the Wye at Chepstow. It may not have been until late 1852 that Newnham gained its station either, as the contract for its construction was let in August of that year. This scene, with both platforms busy with passengers, dates from around 1910. In the bay on the far left is the railmotor for Cinderford and Drybrook. This passenger service started in 1907 and ceased in 1958. Soon after Newnham Station first opened, an advertisement of a house for sale appeared in the *Gloucester Journal*, '*at Coleford, near Newnham on Severn where there is a railway Station*'. The station closed in 1964.

A different form of transport on display here. None of the people in this view have been identified but the car, a Ford Model T, may have belonged to the rather grand looking elderly lady sat in the back or might have been owned and in use locally as a taxi-cab. The George Hotel had dropped the 'Lower' from its name by the time of this *circa* 1920 photograph but it was added again some years later.

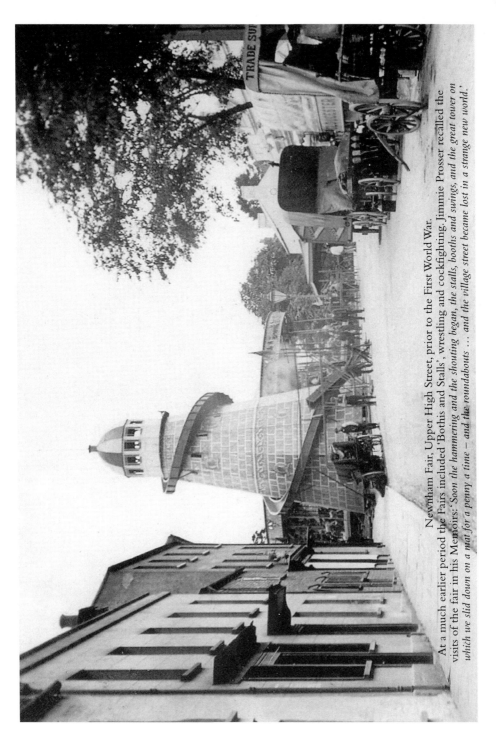

Newnham Fair, Upper High Street, prior to the First World War.

At a much earlier period the Fairs included 'Bothis and Stalls', wrestling and cockfighting. Jimmie Prosser recalled the visits of the fair in his Memoirs: *'Soon the hammering and the shouting began, the stalls, booths and swings, and the great tower on which we slid down on a mat for a penny a time – and the roundabouts … and the village street became lost in a strange new world.'*

Another view of the pleasure Fair, which was the last survivor of the town's fairs. It was held on the Feast's of St Barnabas (11 June) and St Luke (18 October). Newnham's June Fair Day was the traditional day for local farmers to start mowing, even if it poured with rain (why weren't they at the Fair, rain or shine?). Livestock sales at the June fair came to an end during the First World War and Newnham Fair ended in 1928. Here we see W. Symonds Leaping Horses Roundabout in operation. Newnham also had an annual Wild Beast Show, held near the church lych gate. In June 1876 George Sanders brought his Menagerie & Circus. In August that year, J. Philpotts, the chemist, gave a Pyrotechnic display at the end of the holiday amusements provided by Sangers Fete and Gala. Again from Jimmie Prosser's Memoirs: '*The circus came once a year – the procession of the terrifying stilt walkers who could easily peep into the bedrooms brought screams of abuse from the housewifes and young girls… The Menagerie came once a year and I remember the horrid smell of the great beasts, and Macoms the great lion tamer.*'

A celebration at the junction of High Street and Church Road but of what? – the lady's hats are a celebration themselves! A man at the back appears to be wearing medals and the one in front of the drum some insignia, whilst the Newnham Band is also present. There is a boy scout in the picture, which dates it as after 1908, when the scout movement was founded. The Union flags suggest a national event, probably the Coronation of King George V in 1911.

Another Fred Blanton card, from around 1910. The Church of England School in Church Road was built in 1867 and enlarged in 1885 to take up to 250 children. Alfred King was the headmaster in the 1920s, with Miss Jervis in charge of Infants. It closed when the new school in Station Road opened in 1979. There was also a boys private school in Highfield Villas and a girls private school where the Post Office is now.

It was to one of these cottages at the top of Church Road that Jimmie Prosser returned, when he came back to Newnham to look after his blind mother. In his Memoirs, he recalled the Quarter Sessions held at the Town Hall, opposite page: '*The County Court was held in Newnham once a Quarter, and I can see in my mind's eye, the great chair for his honour the Judge being carried by the Bailiffs from the lawyers office to the Town Hall.*' This view dates from circa 1920.

Repairing the wall on Church Hill. There is a theory that the road to Chepstow once ran under the church cliff, alongside the river. However, the road as we know it today existed in the reign of James I, as marked on a map of that period. The hill would have been much steeper then. '*Notice is hereby given. That all persons disposed to treat for Lowering the Hill on the Turnpike Road entering the town of Newnham from Chepstow, by taking off the upper part of the same, and*

raising the Foot of the said Hill, securing the walls on each side ... according to a Plan and Specification thereof, deposited for inspection at the Bear Inn, Newnham ... 1 May 1820.' The repairs shown here were probably before 1914. Random quarried stone was delivered and dressed on the site – drill marks can be seen where the stone was quarried. The varying sized stones in the wall are dressed on the outside only and are called 'shoddies'. The man bending over is Walter Hatton, builder and stonemason.

This view is looking up Dean Road in the Winter of 1947. On the right is the Independent Chapel, built in 1826. By the 1870s, it was in use by the Newnham Volunteers – in 1861 the town had an Artillery Company of sixty men, which was still in existence in the early 20th century. During the 1880s, the chapel was used as a church school and later it became an artist's studio. In the mid 20th century, the local branch of the Plymouth Brethren began using it as a Meeting House. Beyond, facing the camera, is Hill Cottage, which possibly dates from the 16th century. Further up, on the left near the figure on the road, is the Pound.

The Town Hall was built circa 1850 and privately owned, being leased out. The County Court was held here and the cellars were used as cells until the new Police Station was built in 1873. When the lease expired, the Petty Sessions moved to Littledean Gaol. Various other organisations had leases including a Savings Bank and, as can be seen from this pre-First World War photograph, the Forest of Dean Conservative Association had an office here.

Unlawater Corner in the 1930s, dominated by the imposing Unlawater House, formerly Hill House. Mainly 18th century, it stands on the site of an earlier house. Robert Pyrke lived here and later James Wintle, a solicitor in Newnham. In 1908 it became the home of Walburga, Lady Paget, who renamed it Unlawater House. She was responsible for finding a bride for the Prince of Wales, later Edward VII. The two milk churns look like Cadbury churns, which would be picked up by lorry. At this time Newnham had three dairy men delivering milk; George Wickson of Little Hyde and Dean Forest farms; Percy Long who had a dairy at Severn Terrace; and Ben Hinds of Staure Farm. Early every morning, horses pulling milk floats could be seen being driven at a spanking pace up the High Street.

Above: According to Maurice Bent (*The Musical Traditions of Dean*), a brass band was formed in Newnham in 1884. From the style of the dress, it would seem likely that this photograph of the band was taken at that time. They disbanded around 1905 but reformed again as Newnham Town Band in 1909. The bandroom, opened in 1912 at a cost of £20, was along the lane off Unlawater Lane. After struggling financially through the 1920s, the band finally broke up for good around 1935.

Left: Although taken for the bandsmen, in the background of this photograph is the Ship Inn. It was formerly called the Rose but when the Ship Inn on the other side of the street changed its name to the Upper George, the Rose was renamed the Ship. This change of names has led to some confusion regarding the Sanctuary Room at the Ship, which was at the original Ship Inn not the present one. Frederick Baghurst was the publican for over 40 years at the Ship Inn seen here, which was a tied house being owned by the Stroud Brewery Company. The photograph was taken around 1920 and the Newnham Town Bandsmen featured have been identified as George Wellington, 'Leggy' Hooper and Mr Evans of Blaize Bailey. Behind them is the ornate drinking fountain erected in 1897 to commemorate Queen Victoria's Diamond Jubilee.

Just upstream from Newnham the main road was vulnerable to the river's tide and in 1725 the Quarter Sessions ordered the building of a causeway to be protected by a 5 foot wall. This photograph of the road in flood was taken about 225 years later, circa 1950. During the late 1930s, Silver Foxes were bred here. They were kept in a cage on the river side of the road, which is where the name of the cafe, which came later, is derived. There used to be a barkyard near here and Broadoak can just be seen in the

distance. *'The men and women coming home from the barkyards at Ruddle and Broadoak covered with russet brown sweet smelling dust of the bark.'* (Jimmie Prosser, Memoirs). The picture below dates from around 1958 and shows the road and the Silver Fox cafe in sunnier circumstances.

A Church Service on the Cliff – the womenfolk's dresses and the men's straw boaters again mark this down as a pre-First World War occasion. These services were held on what was known as Hospital Sundays. The collection, or most of it, went to the Royal Infirmary at Gloucester. A special service was held at the outbreak of war in 1914.

These two circa 1912 postcard views, by Will Phillips of Gloucester, offer directly opposing views. The top picture is looking along the Green, with a view of the Severn and Bullo on the right. This walk is on top of what is thought to be part of the ancient fortifications of the castle, surrounding the church. The church is out of sight to the left and the railway yards, where the Cinderford branch actually joined the main line, were in the fields to the right of the river. Wagons laden with Forest coal were sorted here for onward despatch, whilst a few were shunted down to Bullo Dock for tipping into one of the small sailing vessels which still occasionally called. The vista of Newnham church and The Nab, below, is taken from Bullo Fields.

This large house overlooking the river was built in 1866-68 at a cost of £10,000 and opened as the Severn Bank Hotel in 1868. Two years later it was in the hands of the liquidators, with full closure and sale of the stock taking place in 1872. That same year it was bought by H.R. Lückes, a Forest of Dean colliery owner, who re-

named it Riverdale. In 1875, Mr and Mrs Edwin Crawshay came to live at Riverdale. In October 1884, human remains were found in the garden. They were thought to be soldiers killed in the affray at Newnham during the English Civil War. In 1901 the house was sold to Captain B. Nilsen of Bath for one tenth of what it cost to build. Capt. Nilsen put the house back up for sale in 1906, producing a postcard advertising it, above, with full details of the house on the reverse, right. It was bought in 1907 by Brightlands School, which then moved to Riverdale and re-named it Brightlands. The school closed down in the 1950s but the property still survives having been converted into flats. The view of the house from across the river also includes the ferry again, with ferryman Tom Phillips standing on the right.

THE HOUSE has been built about forty years, is Detached, and constructed of Red Brick, relieved with Cream and Burnt Bricks. It is of imposing and pleasing appearance, and contains:—

On the ENTRANCE FLOOR—Porch, Entrance Hall (25 by 14), School Room (18 by 14), Smoking Room (20 by 15), Dining Room (27 by 21), Morning Room (12 by 21), Drawing Room (25 by 20), Billiard Room (30 by 20), Ante-Room, Lavatory, Store-Room, Well-fitted Pantry (h. and c.), Large Kitchen, with Hot-water Dresser, Eagle Range and Hot-plate Stove, &c., Larder, Scullery.

Laundry, Coal-house, Servants' w.c., Boot-Room and Larder in enclosed Yard. Principal and Secondary Staircases.

On the FIRST and SECOND FLOORS—Eighteen Large Bed and Dressing Rooms, Bath Room (h. and c.), Lavatories, and Three w.c.'s.

In SEMI-BASEMENT, approached by Two Stone Staircases, are a large Beer Cellar, Two Well-fitted Wine Cellars, Game Larder, and several good Rooms, with Gas and Fire-places, suitable for House-keeper's Room, Servants' Hall and Bedrooms.

THE SANITARY ARRANGEMENTS ARE CERTIFIED. Gas, Hot, Cold and Soft Water laid on.

The principal Rooms open out on to a Balcony, and have lovely Views of the Severn (half-a-mile wide), Westbury, Arlingham, with the Vale of Berkeley and the Cotswold Hills.

The GROUNDS and GARDENS, which are secluded and have fine Trees, comprise about 2½ ACRES. They are well laid-out and stocked. Large Tennis Lawn and Shrubbery Walks.

STABLING is provided for Seven Horses. Good Cottage and Out-buildings, Hot-houses, &c.

Hunting, Boating, Fishing. Anchorage for Yacht. Shooting may be rented.

The Property is FREEHOLD, Free from Ground Rent and Land Tax, and is in Excellent Repair.

Extra LAND could be arranged for if desired.

For further particulars, apply to—

Capt. B. Nilsen.
Riverdale.
Glo. Newnham.

This house near Newnham Pill is partly built of the black blocks, which are very hard and durable. In the 1930s there was a riverside tea garden at the far end of this building.

Newnham Sands in the 1920s – the seaside of the Forest of Dean. People from Cinderford and Littledean walked to Newnham during the summer, to spend Saturday or Sunday afternoons on the sands. After the railmotor service between Cinderford and Newnham started in 1907, the Cinderford

people came by rail. Teas were served at Carefield's Refreshment Rooms and at Burnetts, both in the High Street, and up the steps at the top of Severn Street at the Upper George Tearooms. Later there was a riverside tea garden near Newnham Pill. Now the tides have moved the sands away from Newnham and scenes like this are no more. Note the warehouse again, on the far left.

We end as we started, by the river. The river, always the river, the reason for Newnham's existence, its benefactor and its foe. At high tide, at low tide, fascinating in all its moods. The silver birch trees were planted to commemorate George V's Jubilee in 1935 and the flower beds to commemorate George VI's Coronation. The fish house is just out of picture on the right but Broadoak can be seen in the distance. During the summer in the 1930s a man used to pedal out to here from Gloucester with an ice cream cart. Views of the Severn from the road have been obscured since the embankment to prevent flooding was built and the flower beds have gone. However, the path along the river bank to Hawkins Pill has recently been cleared after being overgrown for many years so it is possible once again to undertake this lovely walk.

BIBLIOGRAPHY

The Victoria County History of Gloucester Vol. X, 1972; Kelly's Directory of the County of Gloucester, 1885, 1902, 1906, 1914, 1931, 1939; Newnham-on-Severn by Mabel K. Woods, 1912; Newnham News in The Papers by Anne Lloyd, 2002; Newnham Banks. History from 1830 by Anne Lloyd, 1994; Memories of Newnham on Severn by J. Prosser, 1963; A New History of Gloucestershire by Samuel Rudder, 1779; History of the County of Gloucester, Vol. 2 by Thomas Rudge, 1803; Men and Armour for Gloucestershire 1608.